I0196492

A TERRIFIC UPROAR

Bolton

ISBN: 978-1-915079-29-9

Cover designed by Aaron Kent

Edited and typeset by Aaron Kent

Broken Sleep Books Ltd
Rhydwen,
Talgarreg,
SA44 4HB
Wales

Contents

I. The Rag

II. The Rite

III. The Riot

IV. The Reality

A Terrific Uproar

Scout Tzofiya Bolton

For my boyfriend; Vaslav Nijinsky.

I.

THE RAG

Moscow Theatre Opens Hamlet

(JANUARY 5, 1912)

The clouds still hang on me, but there's a bravery to my grief.
It's been *like that* with me, always looking for new metrics
With which to grade my resentments, five out of nine criteria;

All around my head, a can-can dance of tipsy bluebirds,
Tiny defibrillators of insomnia (the disorganised type).
Give me some light away. The wind is dashing near my blood.

I felt there like a stranger, hemmed in between a doctor and
His Gladstone bag, a fortune teller with ten carats of peridot
For every other finger; I was just about to offer my palm

But up came the curtains. The rest should have been silence.
I read this wasn't stageable, some creative dissonance backstage,
The scenes and sets all fell down (you'll just have to trust me).

They call it *interference theory*; with every collapsed prop,
I lost another crucial part of me: my birthday, home address,
How to cheat psychometric tests, worship icons, how to talk

To G-d almighty in a music hall for — two long hours?
Two short months? Who can say? I have always lived alone.
A socket, a theoretical cough, a museum.
All other ways are false and dead.

The fortune teller cried, as if offended or surprised, said,
"Sir, you should ask your friends defend you.
I see that you are hurt."

And as I lay face down in the foyer, after falling down
The stairs, I thought:
"You know, that's not the worst advice I ever heard."

The Bolsheviks Gain Independence as a Party

(JANUARY 28, 1912)

After Auden

Like nights of bells and fashionable bounds,
Glaciers they watch by noons, shows of tactic,
Supernatural factions, madmen rallies —
Fevers burn with victory.
Fractions of every farthing each;
All revolutionaries must kiss.

I have an opportunist vision, eager
For the start of any movement,
In arms until the break of day,
Nights of insult, involuntary powers;
Recruit me, please, ferociously.

Pedantic shows of strokes exposed
And all those dreaded graves prevailing
Over boring cries for leadership and salaries,
A thoughtful proletariat, united shows,
The hermit's ambiguous phraseology.
The Menshevik vision, lost.
The bodies and souls of men have no real cost.

Comrades as they lie upon
A bourgeois-democratic thought.
Enchanted Soviets, ordinary;
Considering the eye beautiful.

Mayor Yukio Ozaki of Tokyo Gives 3,000 Cherry Trees to be Planted in Washington D.C. to Symbolise the Friendship Between the Two Countries

(MARCH 27, 1912)

So I bought all the cherry trees in Washington D.C.
Because I believe bloody fruit should be for the many,
Not the few.

Every night my study prays itself a Ma'ariv
In a choir of the sounds smoke makes
And the snow makes
And the rustle of a snare
When you spin it and spin it
Pink moons bristling on the corduroy ground
Like I am tipped and shaken all aglitter
And soaked from a polytonal, years long winter
In a St. Petersburg park, after dark.

Far from the truth, but interesting to note:
Snowstorms are just floods
The weight of a finger; for every blizzard
A soft hand, every fire engine,
Cab-horse, and cynical wayfarer —

Every fibrous glow, a tiny slit still
In my throat from when we all
Drank vodka with real gold in it
That now disperses in blushing grandeur
Throughout my blood.
I might keep one.

TITANIC SETS SAIL

'QUEEN OF OCEAN' EMBARKS ON HER MAIDEN VOYAGE (APRIL 10, 1912)

To old-fashioned people's ideas of swings and pintles, and the hotel. We learn from one, could anything so enthusiastic be as much as a foreign sea? Something better than metric tons of water? Or no dreary slum surrounding The Grand Babylon Royal Automobile Club? The information of splendour with anything else afloat, preoccupied, as we were, with the sea voyage and reception rooms.

Still, to do them justice, left Southhampton for New York in yesterday windows, safely sheltered. Contact at least one small concession. The White Star Liner, with full view of the sea, of swimming baths and electric passenger lifts. Associations more, to most of us, than six or seven storey buildings; *some* of us truly regard the French trelliswork and ivy creepers, parlour sites with private promenade decks a foot thick; the up-to-date appointment of her first Atlantic voyage surpasses the description of the upper promenade.

Contemporary Atlantic passenger. Deck one can peer through. She is 883 feet long, 104 to bridge, and displaces about 60,000; is 90,000,000 miles away, and so many feet deep (or high) from keel. Turkish baths, squash racquets courts, gymnasiums with outer air, astronomers's assurance that the sun and ship make one realise how her rudder is as tall as it tastes of cosmopolitan millionaires, appreciated by the passengers.

Let us, in size and luxury, but especially in Ritz-Carlton restaurants, concert-halls, and Parisian Cafés (in larger Parisian Cafés), and to remote the sea, and its associations with the bridge, displace 60,000 tons of water but especially in luxury. Anything in luxury. In luxury, again — *anything*.

The Titanic Sinks

(APRIL 14, 1912)

No, *you* forgot to cap the bulkheads at the top.
No, *you* ignored the Mesaba's warnings.
You said the ocean was too calm to spot an iceberg.
You forgot to pack binoculars for the crows-nest.
You ordered hard-a-starboard too late,
And *you* went on to let the starboard
Scrape along the iceberg.

You were the liar who said the compartments were airtight.
You were the idiot who said we should reverse the engines.
I said simply bearing left would do the trick,
But *you* thought *you* knew better.
You launched the lifeboats well below capacity
You put 38 too few people on the first one, and actually —

"Posh" never meant "Port Out, Starboard Home".
"Fuck" never meant, "Fornication Under the Command of the King".
"Golf" never meant, "Gents Only, Ladies Forbidden"
You have always said such *ridiculous* things.

The lights went out at 2:18 am,
The nearest rescue ship
58 whole nautical miles away.
But you *knew* that, of course,
Because I told you it was, because
it was me who said:
"The nearest rescue ship is *literally*
58 whole nautical miles away".

A FAWNING AFTERNOON

'AFTERNOON OF A FAUN' BY DEBUSSY IS PREMIERED AT THE THÉÂTRE DU CHÂTELET IN PARIS (29 MAY, 1912)

PICTURED: VASLAV NIJINSKY, PRODIGAL NEW BRAT OF THE BALLETS RUSSES, WENT TO THE LOUVRE AND GOT IDEAS ABOVE HIS STATION

For this I had a box reserved at the opera, where the flute's opening measure rudely suggested I jump to a pinpoint prick in Paris. Could've been anywhere: a road, a river, either and I'd be with all the baubles and shipments and street-lit silhouettes of boys come to carry their pallets of Bordeaux and roses. But I've never been one to listen to flautists, nor bony boys on docks.

So far I've tallied 141 laborious seconds of Nijinsky stretching — whose name I caught for the first time last week from a man with a cane but no limp, and a white shock of hair so much like a skunk that we call him "The Skunk," even to his face, while behind his back we call him *pederast*, straight-backed there in his cordoned space pretending to care one bit about the ballet here and not our leading satyr. Weeping, muted greens on the backcloth, blackest the mound upon which our faun lies prone. Three nymphs with the physiques of Breton pickpockets on the beach move like friezes side-on to a phantasy doped on E major, Nijinsky's faun an amorphous breeze only pegged to the stage by those two great, beating, adolescent eyes. I'm concerned about those leaps. His poor bones. Here, this brandy I cradle balms my calves on his behalf, my hamstring torn by proxy, my doubled pulse on the inside of my elbows, mimicking his, as if a life I've borrowed yet unfolds in my arms. I'd love to say I have a cutesy rabbit-bone metaphor here, that I have no personal contempt for the backstage flaunt of men gossiping like schoolgirls, swapping their directories for business and sport, but I'm here for my quite obvious interest in classical formalism, the noted faux antiquity of the Greeks brought to life. That much is obvious, yes?

Nijinsky rinses breath through these inert antiquities, leaps like a flick-knife drawn at supper, then, flirting about on a long chiffon scarf, like a patriot thanking a flag for its service, I mean *formlessly*, and look. It's not that I don't appreciate the gesture, it's just quite the audacity he's shown us all today, when most people we know wouldn't even begin to *believe* they could live outdoors of their own psychology this way, let alone so nauseatingly, so prettily, as if anyone is really *listening* — still, today a new modern realm of dance came.

Down in the stalls, gaggles of glittering peeresses were hurriedly writing cheques to restore the frescoes.

A Premature Detonation of Dynamite Kills 18 Men Working on the Construction of the Canadian Northern Road, Lake Opinicon, Ontario

(JUNE 2, 1912)

Do we blame the blueprint?
Or hang the architect
Who didn't think
To reinforce the terraces?

Or whoever let the dynamite
Sweat through the dope?

Like two welders welding,
Or two minters lending,
We —

"Daphnis et Chloé" by Ravel is Premiered at the Théâtre du Châtelet in Paris

(JUNE 8, 1912)

It is the Chinese year of The Water Rat
And Gertrude tells me the half-moon
Is waxing in Pisces tonight. I say,
"No, I think it's *waning*", she replies:

"A star of touched dependence has weathered the sky.
A sty. A cylinder. A copied rag, the ballet parades an entire residence.
An echo retracts over highest strength, an echo of echo and strength.
A baggage stripped of danger: this is not true, a stripe of dagger.
Come and say what thinks your afternoon.
Count, count every said you said it says about the dancer.
Stay do you good to take a leave and stay at home tonight.
Nearer than the widening tread, O let's not get about this red kettle.
Show lust has dust in weight and size and nothing ordinary.
Every head you read about the answer, I saw that you saw who.
Accustom your headline sorry formal sorry secretary.
Designated prince, nearly set in where there is a dire pain.
I know that too through you I know that you feel you are through.
I know to you that through you please are what without an answer:
Stay do you good to take a leave, and stay at home tonight and good.
Because your sun is in Aries, your moon is in Virgo,
Vaslav's sun and moon are both in Pisces,
The moon is waxing and furthermore,
We are in a leap year."

"Ha! *Tell* me about it", I said.
But by then she'd got me so drunk,
I wasn't fit to go anywhere.

TOO CLOSE TO THE SUN?

ROBERT PEUGEOT HOSTS PRIZE FOR 'FLIGHT BY HUMAN ENERGY ALONE' (JUNE 20, 1912)

What a great day to gasp at this earnest belief that one man can fly without fuel, nor a motor! Contours of wintry palls winding to aerial towers, informed urbanites naked of intervention would even hazard to say that *this* is how you get to heaven.

The flying craze! 10,000 Francs! not a bad shout for the lucky candidate who ditches his tightrope, cycles ten meters on, and inevitably fails. Still, may he be blessed with the discovery that air has more *give* than one might first assume, I say –

The bike mustn't be a bike in the truest sense of the word. Not a vehicle for descendants of Mars and Hercules. Not a hang-glider because it's too much of a bike. Not a bike because its genius hybrid is sublime. Besides, only the grace of the Bicycle Beautiful could save the amateur hang-glider from the stigma of physical effort, hence why a hairsbreadth from the ground is nothing. Just a ramp to the air of triumph, note stems leaping, tansy thriving in a shaded foreground, men falling down. Splendid organisation; such grace and slender ease.

Suffragettes stood up on their pedals to heckle. One must pad the footholds lightly, like muting an organ; joyfully thumb the dome-bell trigger, a chrome cathedral roof in the palm of one's hand. I see no signs of deterioration, nor rust. Nothing spoiled or lost.

Made like a gun, hung like a pacemaker, built like a bike. High-wheeler, radically right and reasonable. Lightweights make light hearts, fay juveniles. A Matador, all-steel, shipped on approval, an all-grey pelvis nestling the seat, alloy tibia, the gleam of February sun, an attempt at aerocycle, peddling a winged faun for premier, attempts of the handles. Engaged by the legs, a popular press in an alien world. This peach sherbet I lip round the edges of sunrise, one minute earlier per morning. Claret fumes, wood polish. Snow overexposes lawns the land over.

A massive front chain-ring, offset by a cog, air-filled tires on Maple frames (*NB: Are we sure about that?*). Gliding as of another essence from myself (*NB: I almost want to suggest spruce?*).

None of them got off the ground, so Peugeot's running the whole thing again: one tenth of the prize, for 10 centimetres of flight. A patronised Icarus. Pathetic. Unreservedly sad.

Frida Strindberg Opens "The Cave of the Golden Calf" Nightclub nr. Regent Street, London

(JUNE 26, 1912)

In private from all faith,
We put our golden calf in a cave.

Inaudible shadows play against a drop-cloth of raw meat,
Playing cards and wedding rings
Thrown down past nursery hours.
I can just about make out, through a hazy shy
Of Cognac bottles, that there are columns and capitals,
Wall hangings look just like stairs with lolling tongues,
Bile sticky on their molars,
Choking out new radical landscapes
Where Milanese opera singers kick their legs
And men go hunting big game.
Wives and sons ditch their earrings,
Prime the canvas, melt the size
And mix like troubled paint.

Groans of war in campy backrooms,
Handkerchiefs stuffed in our trouser pockets,
Sweet oils on our inner wrists
To radiate our tendencies;
I am a heat. I am *the* heat.
I am a downpour reverberating past sense,
Mad percussionist, roughcast perfectionist,
Pulling off the front with such brilliant audacity
That I have become now a one-man doctrine in reverse;
I should be hysterically kissed, votively fucked,
Let there be limbs flung up against the drop-curtain where
The paints lip wet at the edges,
Slick and snarled up, Primitivist daubs
On our bare backs and knuckles.

The Rite of Spring, that's all anyone keeps saying.
Ford said it, Ezra too, but it was Wyndham
Who sneezed out the name as primary form,
Blood on a tissue:

"Diaghilev, is it true, that under your cheap cap,
Which hides the image of Kephren,
Down past the slick black pomade on your hair,
You had the *presence of mind,*
In the divine name of Youth,
To replace Fokine, in his pink and sky-blue trousers
With one Vaslav Nijinsky, as choreographer
For Stravinsky's new… *thing*?"

And I believe, by complete faith,
That the cocaine (blessèd be thine neurones)
Became my body, one whole, one self in that moment.
May my whole periphery be slaughtered underfoot,
Face warped in the silver tray,
The graduate creations of a hero;
Fragment and void both whipping up to see—

> Jean Cocteau, a lithograph in colour
> (from multiple stones and plates)
> 197cm x 123cm, paper laid on cotton,
> Title: "The Ballets Russes' production,
> *Spectre de la Rose*; Vaslav Nijinsky,
> 1911"

A young beast of prey kept caged in darkness,
Now tipsy in the light of Eden —
And gold called the calf heaven.

I've been working much too hard.
I can't remember the last time I prayed.
Sediments of crushed-up morphine pills
In my desk's inkwells forever.
I drink it down.
Black tongue, black teeth.

As from tomorrow, I take leave.

Joseph Stalin is Arrested at a Masquerade Ball by the Russian Secret Police, and Exiled to Siberia

(FEBRUARY 23, 1913)

I think that I shall never see
A pogrom lovely as a trial.

A triangle whose hungry murder is pressed
Against the winter's sweet flowing breath;

A trend that looks at godsons all deadbeat,
And ligaments of leafy armistices to pray;

A trespasser that may, in summons, wear
A neuter of romance in his haircut;

Upon whose boutique socialism has lain;
Who intimately lives with rampage.

Poetries are made by forfeits like me,
But only G-d can make a trial.

Kaiser Wilhelm Convenes a War Council in Order to Prepare the German Public for a Potential War of "Slavdom Against Germandom"

(DECEMBER 8, 1912)

We had stayed up all night, my friends and I,
Tearing gullies to the sea as traffic rumbled outside.
No ice to sky, nor suddenly struck by fires of one great kiss,
Sentries between him and me, consumed; corroding
Up the city banking.

Praying with the curtains closed, suddenly we jumped,
Rented birds hidden away in hired holiday villages.
A long wait for frost, we had asked for winter, please,
But all we got was locomotives lurching
From inside the earth, launched at us from outdoors
And breeding with mould.

Silence uprooted, an army of engined
Dragons, and the children hid
And mercifully pretty snow had
Graced us from heavenly encampments
Stars plotting out their courses,
Colossal drunkards hulking, took
Rooting on embankments, stoker ships,
Jouncing buoys like eight low candles,
Heckled by the grinding bones of
Omnibus lines, their scorched intestines huge
And ancient crimson, a strange white world;
Feeding the hellish universe is pristine and sickly.

Palaces above the sea,
Car whose hood yelps up a human leap,
The latest beauty; we intend to huddle
If indeed they ever speed, still in meditation
And judgement-hour dignity.

Hurl your pikes and laugh your thinning teeth out
At the necessity of love, and hymns in love
That we intend to sing from side to side,
If you blow up before the wonder of creation
Has its spirit beaten out, we won't exalt explosions,

Praise aggressions, we are men
And underneath such things; for if the men
Lay round like pipes do, and we do,
We will ride on strafe, unthreatening
Round the hooping of eternity
And roar; all men's hearts in the same hour,
Alone, awake and deepened
In rapture and in sleep, across the earth —

Then I'll hold you behind, and at a stoic captain's pace ,
With fearlessness into unknowable centuries.

King George I of Greece is Assassinated by Anarchist, Alexandros Schinas

(MARCH 18, 1913)

He fought so hard to live.
A rose, a rotation, a rouble necropolis.
A taxonomy for the whole farm.
A task for the whole family.
Went walking on a slip-way near a hollow post-mill;
A hollow postman millionaire, a sloop,
A rouge necropolis.

Before rehearsing on a cut-out, one must stimulate
A panorama attempt, a paperback auctioneer.
He fought so hard to live.
Run up and down the stairs twice
To simulate a panic attack,
And then at once rehearse your steady hand.
A tassel for the whole fan.

Spoons and knives in celebration, pies with pig muscle speck,
Black Hand Gang in green-red braids, comrades kiss your sister,
You rally at the altar with contempt for modern regency, Russia,
Europe, and all promenades.
Caveman of a hero, pursuer tiger tapestry:
"We will fight them, we will fight them".
A task for the whole family.
Cease of heterosexual.

The king is dead. Long dead, the king.
A taunt for the whole fanfare.
The rehearsal shoot-out, spoons and knives,
Rally at the altar.

Cavalcades of heritage written on purple ticker tape,
Stuffed inside a balsam bottle, buried near a root.

He fought so hard to live.
A task for the whole family.
Hiding in plain sight in what we now know
Is a necropolis.

STRAVINSKY BALLET PREMIERE

"THE RITE OF SPRING" ARRIVES TOMORROW AT THE THÉÂTRE DU CHAMPS ELYSÉES, CHOREOGRAPHED BY VASLAV NIJINSKY

(MAY 28, 1913)

A dancer is very particular about his work. He dances out every war that will not speak for itself, but no wars that will speak for themselves. I ask: does the dancer dance out his own war? If he does, he can't. If he doesn't, he must. Such a dancer cannot exist. Though a choreographer could.

II.

THE RITE

ADORATION OF THE EARTH

I: INTRODUCTION

An orchestral introduction before the curtain rises.

You whisper from the wings: "Plato called it a *daisy-world,*
Lifeforms self-evolving, the world
Is an eager mental health professional
Brought forth from chaos, as today's version of otherness.

Withdraw with me socially, me: a planet with
No thoughts to own but its own, several of sciences –
I just need a lot more time, I notice these changes in space,
I envision a perfect living system, a personal selection
According to help those in the daisy-world, show changes,
Separate the gods from time immemorial;
False opinions are fancy but more empathetic,
In ways most perfect, our universal fraternity
Questions new ones, severally,
This divine ploughshare cutting a life
That is so perfect, all in our other spirit worlds
And in ways that makes the personal central
And interconnected, malleable, unacceptable realities:
We are going to dance the earth out.
Not yet, but we are going to dance the earth out."

No he *didn't,* Vaslav. There are no interpersonal dimensions,
You just have unusual, over-valued thoughts.
More than anything else we should consult together
In the gatherings of psychosis,
And in the furrows of whimsy.
Though I'd love to withdraw with you,
You are far too delirious.
And sometimes you sound like a communist.
A swarm of spring pipes transcribed from ancient scrolls
Foretell that earthquakes are just wisdoms screaming to get out.

II: The Augurs of Spring

A celebration of spring stirs on the horizon. A fortune teller has bad news.

Tears or thrilling snap of pleasure
Lower back in pear-tree structure
Leaping wheels, bird-in-the-hip,
Mayday mayday ankle strain or
Thrush-wing plié's soft contusion,
Primrose prone of labral fracture,
Repeated impacts in Eden's garden
And periwinkle disc degeneration.

Move through the music and not against it.
We must love one another or die.

My heart to my toe, aggrieved
And lying flat, the blue breath in the
Lowest man and spring's glassy fan
Above me, all I can do when heaven,
Renewed, pets my legs awhile,
Is thank the hairline fracture in
My thigh for how it came to be.
That was how I came
To unlearn dance itself:

We broke our ankles, bled through our tights —
Our gratefulness presumed, as some of us *were.*

Less a simple Narcissus than a complicated Androgyne,
An odder orchid dewed with feminine fluency —
Please let's protect this curious, good and purest thing;
Pure for being unlike man, because he is not human.
Pure for being inhuman, because he is a genius.

His removed, gracile strength,
And it only cost two silver francs for his masseuse
To give me a briefing of his musculature,
And even sang it to me gladly at no extra fee:

"Don't expect of him any less than full-time elegance.
His positively naked Rose is proof of Messianic thought!"

That's why I can't think your name in any house of G-d.
You have made His earth the perfect dwelling place.

Baruch attah Adonai Eloheinu, melech ha'olam shekahacha lo bo'alamo.[1]

1 "Blessed are you, our G-d, King of the Universe, who has such beautiful things in his creation.

III: Ritual of Abduction

The young girls arrive in single file, straight from the river.
They begin the ritual of dancing the abduction.

Rays were gunning through the atmosphere of the earth.
I saw a horseshoe and took it as a portent, an oratorio
Gradually passing into all the colours of rave;
From lightning bluebird to darkroom blush
To virginal and then to black;
An indescribable gamut of colours
Just like the pallbearers of assailants,
Their motives flaming through the aubergine of eclipse,
Crude embolisms, daisies, atonal and polytonal
Pile-ups, counterbalanced –
The estrangement of striving to far-off worlds
Is embodied by assimilation
And our lightness in them,
A wholehearted fellowship, The wraith of pursuit,
Final assent to your Okhrana thumbscrew,
And this is not easy whilst debutantes, heretics,
Hypochondriacs and forgeries sweep like foresters
About us; they are stupid, they are beasts, they are meat,
They are death:

How can you now talk so simply without any affectation?
I just don't know how any more.

IV: Spring Rounds

The girls of the tribe ritually dance the Khorovod.

The telephone rings and rings.
People run and run.
He does not know who is calling or what they are calling about,
Because he does not like talking on the telephone.
A backspace, a pale image, multiplying.

It's more than that, it's constant.
Holy painted mountains, teenaged
And regenerating; a saint stamping
Up and down at different speeds then
Pulls the ground, play and pretend
The divots there, dragged by a bull.
Everybody thinks that he is ill.
He bellows, but he is not a bull.

They just keep arriving, state frontiers
The whole terrestrial globe.
His face looks
Like a mask, a new planetary transit
Makes me speak in rhyme because I am
A rhyme. All astronomers are stupid.

What childhood taught us both becomes our circuitry.
Frantic exposure, our spirit rails a rumour.
A chair thrown through the industry window.
An unconnected pattern.
In some ways this is intercourse,
Like two conflicting motorways
In violent, changing layers,
This bastard panic,
Some creature cracks,
His muscle overflows against
An overlooked cosmology —

He likes Jews with short hair.
I love him but I do not understand him.

V: Ritual of the Rival Tribes

The tribe divides into two groups now in opposition to each other, and begin the 'Ritual of the Rival Tribes'.

We coexist in regression / I coexist in regression
There is me / And the double in me
A mirthful obliviousness / Irreconcilable wishes
One consciousness / But the pin is not felt.

The dominant behaviour / Major hysteria
Sidestepping responsibility / Childhood states
A brief transitional struggle / A swoon or a slump
The alternate other / Is more anaesthetic
So a strong jab with / The pin is not felt.

A trance state of 24 hours / I told you I was stabbed
Caused by the death / Of the parish priest
Then baby appears / We teach him to walk
He watches their feet / Imitating his elders
Though he sees he is bleeding / The pin is not felt.

Contact is controlled / Tact is controlled
The spell is broken / Development impeded
A negative zero-order / Emotionally detached
One degree of sulking / Garden at dusk
The superego / Thrown in mischievously
An unknown hand / The girls disappear
Catch one another / A moderate game
Play is warm / In the nocturnal depths
I see I am bleeding / But the pin is not felt.

VI: Procession of the Sage

A holy cortège precedes the wise elders of the tribe.

Find THE HIEROPHANT in your Tarot deck. Place him down face-up. Shuffle the deck. Using divination, you can now ask THE HIEROPHANT what you need to know. The cards that answer your questions will leap out of the deck. Those are the cards that will help you.

What is the next step?
The Knight of Disks.
The fire of earth. The lord of the phenomena of mountains who sends earthquakes and gravitation, the activity of earth as a giver of life. The science or practice of farming, including cultivation of the soil. The next step is working with nature, reliably. Form a deep connection with Mother Earth. Maintenance, stability and eternal value. Show philistine enthusiasm, passionate power associated to the deer motif. Help encourage a strong sense of cohesion, attachment, lively and warm sensuality.

What do I have to change?
The Fool.
You are too curious, too interested in experimentation, too hungry for change, your altruistic idealism and infinite imagination may lead to the negative disintegration of structures and imperatives, your goals are too ambiguous, wrapped up in illusory fantasies. Change how childish and irresponsible you are. A gaze glides through everything in a state of not looking. This is a curse. The first spiral is a bunch of grapes. The second is a pigeon, a butterfly, two snakes wrapped around one another. Babies, flowers, the sun. A crocodile and a tiger. A brilliant light on the boundary of appearance; do no look at it, not even once.

How can I change this?
The Ace of Disks.
Numerology: No. 1 (Monad), perfect unity with no dimensions of its own. The pure potential of Kether (Hidden Intelligence). Be complete as a self. Work on the tangible rather than the abstract. Send Earth Energy and you heard me. Help the joyful nature of Mother Earth! The Daisy World! Open Sesame, that's what I'm hearing. Open up open up open up open up open up open up open up open up open up open up.

What do I have to continue doing?
The Knight of Cups.
There are Hebrew associations and Jews do not believe in hell:

ה (female): window opening; aperture; desire; to be; sighting of a star; to breathe; to become.

ו (male): that which joins; nail; peg which holds door curtain before the Ark of the Law; an erection.

ה (female): see above.

י (male): right hand; fist; handle; pointing index finger; hand as a symbol of G-d; power and activity; semen.

Represent self, a horse jumping over a peacock jumping over a horse jumping ping over peak a peacock k acock se jumping over a send horse ping jumpe help a hock pe hove a hovea jumping ove hove or jumping jumping send jumping help jumpin in hock pe pe pe peak

How my life will change as a result of this next step.
The Four of Disks (ill-dignified).
You're not going to share enough of what you have, are you? You're going to use material success as an end in itself, aren't you? You're greedy. You are too insecure about the monetary value of your future. You are sticking to the letter of the law without empathy; an end in itself, aren't your future, you are sticking to what you have, are you? Are you? You? You're greedy. You? You're greedy. You are the letter of the law without going, you're not going to share enough insecure about the monetary future. You? You use to about in your without sticking what the going You as of letter enough and greedy. Enough, you greedy. To are are to you? Are to you? The material you're of an itself, of too not share value aren't have, are monetary going the law your success your insecure end. Your insecure end.

I am the birth of the ~~divine~~ baby Horus. Supernal Triangle and remaining sephira. 'Hearing' from above and transmitting it without bias. Snake and dove around window. Send nails. Rose. Cherubs but in corners. Help geometric shapes. A staff. You know what everyone thinks of you, don't you? I do and if you're not careful, I'll turn the next card over. It feels like The Lovers.

VII: The Sage

The sage brings the dancing and games to a halt, and kisses the earth.

Hand.
The highest form of Mercury.
Get illumination (lamp).
Head looking back (action).
Orphic egg colour of Venus (green).

Pyramid: formed by a top white ray.
Lower white ray: the horizon.
Inner world: outer world.
Subjective: creator.
Objective: man.

Head forward, mouth open.
Middle head.
Prudence fruits.
Wheat. Virgo. Persephone.
Diamond lantern.
Yellow rays from lantern.
Understanding a kind of island.
Pollenating creation.
Now kiss: do not let me.

Help is on the way.

VIII: Dance of the Earth

Everyone breaks into a delirious dance, sanctifying the earth euphorically united as one with everything.

Is the barrier degenerate, are there cheat-codes for doctrines?
There is arsenic in the middle, but never staying there.

Is it like a universal fraternity, or more a fussy chandelier?
It's a pulse like rams in Russia, being interned as forced adoption.

Is there such thing as a love immemorial, or mitzbar?
An unrivalled doomsday, proportions stäk on bed.

Is the windmill to the west of you? Is it fortune or algorithm?
It's a godless revolt, a hearse, a purple rote; I love a good dare.

Dare the ambience hard, then, and I for we new brazen?
Caveman and airborne, and I mitzbar your chauffeur.

A whole purge, Rist Vaslav? Like a church, but a face?
Oh fantasq completely, and axemuscle propole.

Please go propole? Mitzbar salter down, thromb?
Go to Atadachausach; then armsenik that here-atze.

Gole fantasq, quist axemuscle, but when atze thromb?
If rousle fornsid, then tächen hetwest yorgh un kread, int.

We quist plate, Nijinsky, but whostive hare Direback?
Vestay Direback mähsten, cheiyen stäk or dec'tat hetwest.

Unded far creason, so kread int armsenik?
I um G-d, mod G-d undeschen flesh kreadür.

Net, unded far-creason. Net, but far-creason axemuscle.
Propole, stäk un stäk propole fantasq tachen thromb.

Whostive please, for kreadüst *please,* pity me thromb?
Rist salter tachen an ind tachen thromb, um -

Propole, whostive. Ist've sayzen propole. Bret—
Rist salter tachen, ind tachen thromb.
Direback Vaslav um salter, ind stäk: Kreadüst.

THE SACRIFICE

I: Introduction

STAND (IF YOU ARE ABLE)

עימדו אם אתם יכולים.

I believe, in complete faith, in the existence of the Creator, who is perfect in every manner of existence.

אני מאמין, בלב שלם, בקיומו של הבורא, שהוא מושלם בכל צורת קיום.

I agree to pray over a period of time **(period of time)**

אני מסכים להתפלל לאורך זמן (לאורך זמן)

May His name know me, whatsoever, at all. There, let me sympathise all the time, and shoot with, help, exalt forever, both those who dance first and those who dance last. **(Exalt forever)**

שהשם יידע אותי, בצורה כלשהי, בכלל. שם, תן לי להזדהות כל הזמן, ולירות עם, לעזור, להלל לעד, גם את אלו שרוקדים ראשונים וגם את אלו שרוקדים אחרונים. (להלל לעד)

That I will transgress Them with love **(we transgress them)**

שאנו נחטיא אותם באהבה (אנחנו מחטיאים אותם)

I believe it is written: who fashioned us all, who truly cares in the love of humanity, O Vaslav **(love of humanity).**

אני מאמין שזה כתוב: מי שעיצב את כולנו, שאכפת לו באמת באהבת האנושות, הו ואסלב (אהבת האנושות)

I will believe that Vaslav's thoughts are accompanied by His actions. No I don't **(Yes we do)**

אני אאמין שמחשבותיו של ואסלב נלוות על ידי מעשיו. לא אני לא (כן אנחנו כן)

I believe that there is Him. I believe there can be no immortals that come without warning **(come without warning)**

אני מאמין שיש הוא. אני מאמין שלא יכולים להיות בני אלמוות שבאים ללא אזהרה (באים ללא אזהרה)

In perfect faith I believe things are essential because they grow. I believe in this with the most of trouble **(most trouble)**

סירבדש ןימאמ ינא המלש הנומאב
ןימאמ ינא .סילדג סהש ללגב סיינויח
בר ישוק) בר ישוקב הזב)

I believe that for others, if anything else, Blessed be their tolerance to the Rite, for their names, for their possessions, for the whole of them forever and ever **(If anything else)**

רבד לכ סא ,סירחא רובעש ןימאמ ינא
סקטה רובע סתונלבוס ךורב ,רחא
רובע
סתומלש רובע ,סשוכר רובע ,סמש
רחא רבד לכ סא) דעו סלועל)

And I believe this is free, good friend. I believe my good friend is a Divine beauty, may any physical comparisons be cursed upon you (**I believe this is free**)

ינא .רקי רבח ,סניח הזש ןימאמ ינאו
יפוי לעב אוה רקיה ירבחש ןימאמ
לע ללוקת תיזיפ האוושה לכש ,יהולא
סניח הזש ןימאמ ינא) ךידי)

And Yes I believe in the highest forms of being. I will refer to Him as a teacher. In charitable acts and deep love for my fellow lovers I will reach a profound understanding; the body of the prophet **(the body, the body)**

תוהובגה היווהה תורוצב ןימאמ ינא ןכו
ישעמב .הרומ לאכ וילא הנפא .רתויב
סיבהואה ייער רובע הבר הבהאו הקדצ
איבנה לש ףוגה ;הקומע הנבה לא עיגא
ףוגה ,ףוגה)

I pray for the coming of the daisy-world. I believe in the resurrection of the dead **(thank you, Vaslav)**

לש ואובל ללפתמ ינא
תייחתב ןימאמ ינא .תינגרמה-סלוע
בלסאו ,ךל הדות) סיתמה)

II: Mystic Circles of the Young Girls

The young girls engage in mysterious games, walking in circles.

Steel audiences,
black and white, queens
are jealous of my inventory. With
my eyes closed, only your side will dawdle
by the fountain's silver tears, will not meet
your / my / your / my arms and hands, catching
array when your trade meets my chest like pearls, a
spectre or a work-force of sexuality from paradise,
celestial insect smokestacks in ceramic; that's the you
in me, a rose packaged for a rose packaged for this, now
you should sleep, returned from ours, mind not up
yet, still drawn blinking, white and blinking,
cannot quite configure, vital alloy elements,
the Russes in Paris, nouveau tendrils
conjuring you to life;
but strange.

Imagine my
corsage, just *imagine*
my corsage, his and his asleep,
away from you I've plummeted and will
again, visions of impact, such enchanting
products, charming pistons, it's horribly erotic,
me first then you yield again, superbly seminal,
labour me a life of fairest blooms, if I could engineer a
rose: petals indefinable, Paris crimson rusts around my
caskets engraved daily, tombs engraved for days,
and of ourselves: a parallel spinet, I mean a
virgin, I mean a harpsichord, I mean long
and with a fate like mine whose
death is as is, or was as
was, a funeral for all

my dreams
in textiles, dreams in
retail and shipbuilding, and
my rose who would not die for ten
whole enterprising minutes, a poet out the
window, rescue you from ballet and the phantom
men in their refinery rooms, I can't believe your eyes
like beetles, come terrestrially all down my Cocteau
poster of you, laid here with me again I have come
ready-made, a grief now I should leave, but
your body is a warm one. Weld my tears
and let me stay and raise a kiss to
you: here lies not a mass nor
a hymn nor a ball and nor
a floor-cloth curling;
like the art of

him: rose
immortal
who was
there —

and of his bliss,
which was ten minutes
and is still
here.

III: Glorification of the Chosen One

One of the young girls of the tribe has been selected by fate and has been caught in the khorovod twice. She is now honoured as The Chosen One.

this is impractical
fifteen minutes
a dream how you
rifle, a spectacle,
order, some
god? a cowl, a lion
was his comrade

legs crossed on the
ground it's a choice
being around
me or pride it's
pretty well I tried
well
so take the area
chamber music
means tender
dles
in Russian
ed
you
good and
around whenever
you want is
communism
pity me or I die
art is free

also someone's trying four weeks
before leaving bare and blinking
dive into guardian, an aria, a lyric in a
a joke about a bishop, physics and holy
where else he sees a red ribbon, what
a safe hand, social money, said that Isayev
in masturbation he does not sit with his

ground, he said many times in the back
yeah you don't say see don't pray me into
be fascinated did you allocate a parade for
your work sounds like no causes are
in the bath I tried the cocaine I tried the stair-

and fill the area with usually a racehorse or
a foreign piece of hip or length of shin *Nejinka*
and silver icons like to dress thin selling can-

church services until your dancing deteriorat-

know you'll only be assassinated when you're
ready therefore murderers can follow you
they think *Nejinka* means masturbation but all
to be tender masturbation is not at all
and yes i tried that too
inoffensive
and life paralysing.

IV: Evocation of the Ancestors

In a brief dance, the young girls summon the ancestors.

At midnight a person may take a shadow as a ghost, but in the early part of night, this may not be the case. You shot the hats off of people passing in the street; at parties you can be found sitting in the corner, staring at your hands, at all costs.

Then at midpoint a persona may take a shaft as a ghoul but in the early particles of nightmares this may not be your casino; the best throw of the dice is to throw them away, a fool and a thief, the overthrow of a dictator is a footstep and a thorn; staring at your handcuffs, in all cottages.

And the best thing of difference is when, with a migraine, a persuasion takes shame as a gift, but this partnership of nimbuses may not become too casual. A fantasia in a tinderbox. Pastimes have you skiing with a corpse.

The pathologist has found you sitting in the corner, staring at your hands. You shutdown the heads from the perimeter of strongholds. The decaying throes of dignity; a forearm and a thrill, but in these easy pastel nocturnes, our cataclysm:

Me, stroking your hair on all couches.

V: Ritual Dances of the Ancestors

The chosen one is now entrusted to take care of the sages.

A white candle half-over from a forgotten event;
Something you were given on a boat;
Hair in an envelope;
The best sex of your life as a Roman coin;
A slim volume of special words;
A love that breeds horror on sight.

A chest clatter with an echo that was a reverb or the end,
This isn't some kind of ceremony, Doctor,
The cold water you have thrown on it,
I felt it from the other country, even.
The blonde-haired ghoul, contorting/dislocated;
O bent ballerino of mine

Who teases the ozone and kisses the highest tips of earth,
Sets down on land without eye contact in the sheer, membrane
Uniform of the dead, when weather flirts back;
O sly, winking bootlicker of mine.

From old barns and dry-rock walls and frames,
Hide you and seek me footing round the foundations
For memory's sake, but far too half-something to get you.
To get to you.
Exceptionally soothing, the dainty playtime you allow me,
Your head so cool and clammy;
O anomalous heatstroke of mine.

Reams upon reams of lunatic accusations
This burnt heart cross I am branded with.
A small thing, but proper, when an asteroid lands in big water.

The other room is now another route; a swap,
You take my death to dance your own,
Untouched, crooked jaw, I wish I could change
The colour of your lip so I can rub
It with the hallowed grit of where you were born
And where you will later die,
Lick my sooty palms and make inroads in them,
And watch your name whizz by me,
These visits just like rainfall;

O unsettled dark firmament

O boy-on-boy visual

O whipping hound

O bruised clavicle

O dead attic rapture

O giving me head and looking straight up

O puppy dog eyes

O kneeling celebrity

O beautiful plaything

O precious apprentice

O ectoplasm on my stomach

O heavenly ruin of mine.

VI: Sacrificial Dance

The chosen one dances the Sacrificial Dance, watched by the elders, until she dies of exhaustion.

THE NEW RITUALISM: A MANIFESTO FOR ATTACHMENT

You will say nothing to one another that does not confide something. You will not say, "that which has sprung from the ground and became everything", you will simply say: *"we have found our place in the daisy-world".*
Put yourself to work, dismiss psychology for sudden liberation.
No sentimental animal is going to be impressed when you try to shirk the responsibilities of deep admiration by chopping your own body into pieces.

Have the decency to say PLEASE when you are propitiating the gods of Spring.
When you become an article of gold or bead or turquoise say THANK-YOU.
When you ascend to chieftain or monarch and are handed your scythe, you will tell one another immediately and if you don't, the Rites CANNOT take place.
If you do not break into nervous laughter we will intervene ANGRILY.
Use neither fortune teller nor hierophant: do NOT ask for help ANY MORE.

The earth will nourish you and if it refuses then you must return to it by way of an apology to the below-place of Atadachausach. When tunnelling through the mantel you will be fantasq amongst the other Direbacks as Kreadüst expects of you, and you will do so with dignity and propole; NOT bellowing like a bull. You must mitzbar with devotion.

It is not necessary that your intimate relationships should rely on music, but if they do rely on music, that music must be such as it will disgust the expert. Let the neophyte dance in ways that which a choreographer could not describe.

According to all living minutiae you may gain supernatural powers, you can preserve the world's first dawn and remember: there has only ever been one dawn.
You will agree that Biblical lessons are both immediate and delayed.
You will be a master of compassion and of your craft (your love for one

another); you will join together in such a way that your devotion can be called polyphonic and assonant.

You will come to understand miracles, the afterlife, and try not to define the paranormal powers of the workings of your hearts; you will use symmetry to translate religion into harmony.

The idea that the subconscious transmittal of thoughts is what underpins these rituals is the worst thing you've ever thought and you need to stop thinking it. Be sure to be impressive, effectively and quickly, make a drug of yourself, make a target of yourself, a strange and bizarre person, erotomaniac fantasies will feel misguided but you must perceive them as an actress would perceive herself as Cleopatra, you must wait to be assassinated and only then will you be secure that it will never happen, you must be exciting news and warranted, you must be associated with terrible beliefs –

There is something of the ancient about you.
Something very phenomenal about you.
You will dance now to death, and gladly.
This is how you be in love –

ENOUGH.

III.

THE RIOT

Three snorting beasts, minor royals I'm told,
Scream, *"ta gueule!"* at the stage, actually scream,
And I wonder; well, whatever happened to a *quiet* life?

All my tomorrows on peeling window panes,
Crickets shucking from a wet bag of cocaine,
A reliable job, visiting friends on the coast,
And the sound of absolutely nothing.

If I gun-fight myself over what mutation of love
Was the hardest of all, what flavour of hope
Was the sourest, with gossamer networks
Hanging over my head, weaving out big thoughts,
Breeding and hatching, in bed, early morning
(4 down: arachnid, 6 letters.)
And I smack them on the back of l'Epoque with Kandinsky
Then I am doing so alone, and that's mine, and it's private.
Romance and lampshades, a good cruet set,

The decency of dead legs calmer than heartache,
This mass-produced bamboo screen with a few minor crudités
(Added so my mother cannot separate it from handiwork),
That's an appropriate life at my age.
Something proper about killing spiders
With newspapers.
But I have wondered…

That hypothetically our ornament would be
asymmetrical, principally floral, incongruous,
With such *gorgeous* motifs.
Did you ever read what I wrote when I called you a flick-knife?
I meant the two of us in bed, your mother on the line
Asking if you'll give her exactly three grandsons,
And if I've learned anything from my trip to the moon
It's that watching the earth rise in the distance
Is more exhausting than not.
I'll tell her my sister wants to carry your brood
If you'll tell me I'll die with a vivid fray around me
Lucent and sore, muted by sundown
A thick, heavy sleep, a cold pillow.
A secret and dirty and ugly new habit;
Having bricks in my bed.
Having love for those bricks.

A Duchess next, spinning her pearls round her neck
With the frenzy of a dog trying to bite its tail
And she catches them in air like dandelion clocks
And hurls them at the stage in hope
That the dancers will trip and die.
Actually die.

Be my true-crime darling passed out on the lawn,
Wherever we'll go in an hour doesn't matter
Because *please* I'll be driving you into the ground
In the mud slightly heaving with the tiny lives in it,
I'd *die* to take you once on the duck-down,
Kill to have you twice over the bidet,
Then you get shot to death in the bathtub,
I paint it and now

I'm a famous lover of all people, and am
Loved by all people, now I'm a silk hand-fan,
Now I'm nude descending the staircase twice,
Now I'm the Archbishop of Lyon.

The doctor tips out his Gladstone bag in the stalls
And stamps his stethoscope and rectal thermometer to death.
The crack, the noise alone, is enough to feed our beasts.

I'll say, "The bloomy flower water wants changing!
Please take my boots from the corridor for polishing!"
You'll skip to those tones of submissive companionship,
Something to copyright; imagine my teacup,
And your teacup,
Both chipped a little bit.

I hear great discipline is needed to weave a Hepplewhite chair
Such as the one that I bought you, if you noticed, in the hall.
Greater discipline, I will learn, to thaw you out in it,
Tie your wrists to it, glad arms bowing outward
In infinite recursion
As burglars break in through the window,
Lacerating their necks.
I love comedy. I love smoking.
I love drinking in the morning.

I read Freud last night because I had that dream again;
A bicycle flying over Paris, a hierophant,
A fruit bowl with nothing but lychee and lime,
A fine trip for madeleines but now we're all wet,
How cyanide smells of marzipan,
And gypsumweed of liquorice,
Then we both die eating pralines
At the house of Chanel—
Like it was *nothing*.
It turns out there's a fantasy in me,
And it's at least a little bit charitable.

I've been waiting to see you forever.
To be sitting extremely upright in these seats,
These red seats, these red velvet seats,
I've been desperately in need to be sat up, and redly;
Nerveless as a cat-call, impervious as a crocodile,
A firebird psychedelia in the thick of my hip
Where my bone marrow lives if you need it someday.
I don't know if you'll get cancer,
But my liver, too, is waiting.

I expect the rioting aristocrats think
Mythology and the mystic ideal are defeated at last,
But with all their scarves and handkerchiefs wagging in the air,
A centaur could plausibly bust out from the wings.

I note: *overcrowded, fussy, Baroque elaborations.*
You undertow my repression,
Field what's novel about my wristwatch —
Indistinguishable from Europe.
Indistinguishable from portraiture.

The fascinating part of my breakdown is its weekday nature.
A sort of kidney-dish-on-a-nightstand cease of tradition and power.
It *wants* you to feel unsettled.
I *want* you to lien on my lot.
You are my first augury of budgerigars and sirens,
And I'd forgive you for disregarding me as fear.
Just about.
There's a silk rose petal in my pocket, sweet boy.
Apparently I'm a thief as well as everything else.

I was there when you came on the nymph's scarf, that night.
A twelve minute affair and you spent one of them ejaculating.
If a tree looks yellow to me then it's a yellow tree,
If our faces clash then it's not an unfaithful impression,
You taught me a tennis ball can lead to a threesome in *Jeux,*
Petrushka was a sorbet post a culminating sunset,
Fists clenched, depicting the basket,
If a tree looks yellow to me, then I shouldn't have to see it
As anything but

I'm not forcing the issue down the Avenue Montaigne,
Not going to *go on* about how I see the shadow of death
In the shape of all hatstands these days,
Staying with my great aunt for the next several wars;
The height of fashion, a treaty, an eye cut in two.

I am not G-d but the world has been created by G-d.
I am not flesh but I have flesh in my heart- hang on,
Have you seen this?
I like to present interesting things
(and I have for a while, but you will learn this of me),
So look here, for a second:

This alley of beautiful boutiques,
These reinforced steel beams,
These very thin walls,
The big window of the soul,
There are friezes, curving balconies,
A Vaslav every other seat,
Divisions into boxes,
But where's the orchestra?
I can't see the orchestra.
Just a mystical gulf between me and you,
Between me and the rites,
Just face up to it like I've had to –

That we are living in a Jewish zeppelin tonight.
All too German, much too tonic.
Great for a post office
But in no way Parisian.

It doesn't have to ruin my evening,
I'll just move like a block, on top of a block,
On top of a block, in uptight arousal
Those jerking, jolting rhythms
Will be called *derivative* someday
But that bassoon being strangled is so exposing and high,
How obscene to rip the sinew from a Latvian wedding march!

I never thought I'd watch a fortune teller
Start a fist-fight with a duchess.
I've never heard a screech so well received
Until tonight.

Wind like this seems a violent sort of courage,
Bravery eternal, an omnipresent hymn,
Capturing and breaking down the bullying electricity of space,
A new life in attack, shivery insomnia, mortal leaps;
The poet will sit as a corpse and nobody notices.
I hate the absolute. I hate the earth.
I hate crooked lines, thoughtful movements,
I hate beautiful ideas and our own inner libraries,
Polyphonic tides about great bunkers underground.
The work, that by riot, is worth dying time.

Just now the whole orchestra got beat like a drum
Because it bent down to be and said *thank you,* Vaslav.
A small set of binoculars just about misses my head
And that couldn't possibly be fire I smell, is it?

Or is it?

Imagine how funny it would be
If I burned to death in my seat
For refusing to leave —
I am already seeing our lives before our eyes:

Every grace, an explosion of mysterious doors,
Blazing with war, a circle of cars, ancient feelings,
Apes but resembling smoke-plumed serpents,
Multicoloured speed, mimicry gymnasts,
Brides over moons, exalted new beauties,
Nijinsky Nijinsky Nijinsky my atmosphere:

Planes as patriotism, essential militant beauty,
And we enthusiastic must spend the accidental
Leafing through our feelings with utilitarian cowardice,
Up along the way, just on my sleep, you toss
Your spirit astride me, inward, flights of thoughts,
I will adorn you with principles,
Because I have sung this entire period.

Offer me please your sympathy,
Apologise to me, about this,
The revolution, about primordial magnificence,
That dance can lead to danger,
And danger leads to sculpture,
And all sculptures are masterpieces
And that you have made hooves
From classical artistic virtue *en point,* Vaslav —
Knock-kneed Lolitas jumping up and down.

We don't always have to be true to the natural world
So if you turn to me flatly, all elements of depth
Disemployed in the service of your role, if you *have* to,
Then I shall still be ritually devoted to your terms.

But if I threaten to leave the hall?
And take my spleen with me?
Spew my woolly inwards outwards
Like knitwear on the fang-masks
Of the folksy archaical art, in unstoppable accretion?
You have left me with soft eyelashes, bruised wrists,
Living in the frayed-knots drawer of my childhood home.

Rich oriental scarves now ripped up and soaking.
Over there, a mother comforts her crying, adult son.

The very best of us is ugly and lumpen.
The very best of us all is inhuman and mechanical;
I wish we could be

Ringing in its prime key from right to left in ochre drapes,
Marionettes in opera boxes, celluloid, dissociated,
My fingernails clacking together like cockles trying to kiss,
And severance of time and all hours that are bronze,
I will cast this net of intent in secret from my eyes

And maybe they'll all slip and slide and tumble,
Like I should slip and mill about there,
Oh fractal patterns on the walls now,
Fractional holes in the floor now,
Factorial and wholesome, my factions of prose
Origins and termini, opera lights through eyelids
Look like spheres of afterbirth
A rolling timpani snaps off and I have now hired it as kindling

And you were liquid with me and I am all around contusions
Of your resurrection; thoughts are blooming out
Onto the jute cloth wrapped around her ankle, screaming

Wide awake and screaming just like we all are,
Baby Vaslav, beneath the blinding ocean where
We oxidise to sharp confetti,
A rusting bus and you there at the wheel,
Because hell is a shy machine, a scarlet racket,
A topical drug, a revolutionary culprit,
A wide cylinder, a countryside satellite,
A vice trumpet, an antique lips and cheek if you like,
A clock with no arms, they call it a swastika,
And hell is a delirious silver monolith.

The dancers and their sweet, raging wrists,
Tongues like strawberries and every voice a road
In a conspiratorial traffic azure, a trash can of small
And then even smaller ladders
Cantilevering down, I want to leave

Or hang about like a heavy French perfume
Where G-d will mooch around in suede and silk-lined shoes
Oh lick the blooming snow-drop like a continental ice-cream,
An engine lowered from the sun in one whole basket
Kept intact: coughing near an assassinated king and queen,
Moderately tearful, investing in oxygen,
My prevalence like liquor, spoilt apples, an appendix;
This purge is not gibberish, I am a cult ashamed for being one.
But you, a glossy firework, hilarious abuse,
A detective in a chamber, a post-tennis hand-job, and
From what I see is what I know and what I know to see is this:

Vaslav Nijinsky! Covetous as trusts, repelling thunderstorms and noxious, bioluminescent, fuming milk-white bouquets of stagnant luxuries, squealing essences of abominations, of neptunian frosts and winterboundly smacking sights, of peculiar hyacinthine stars! Overheating and crackling, metallic, graceful and only a *little* bland, he is the dry cello over velvet peneplains and quiet saffrons on the eyelashes of giants both livid and fluffy, savoury, acidic, he is a crying pulsar, a sickly dejectedness, agonisingly padded like thrum thrum thrum **thrum** **thrum** and the black insides of a kick- drum! As undivided as petrification! The icy flavours at a minimum, an oceanic trench and white cratered landscapes, the upper tangent arcs and ecstatic silences, palpable grief! Delightful sooty black notes and the glitter! PLEASE the agony PLEASE the machine in me the machine OF me and history like a dull thick burnet and history like a serrated antipathy my solar plexus is combusting so APOLOGISE TO ME I mean I'm sorry I really am I do not even know what words mean so how can I pass judgement? Let the postscript rot below, let *nothing else* survive, oh world! Oh music! Oh art oh love oh love oh love oh FUCK—

I wish I could die in the lung of this fucking thing.
Die speculative
I could die too clear and too clean
Painlessly indefinite
I wish I could die factory made
Die a democrat
Die an irrelevant promotion of myself
Die word-bound like a clever animal
Incessantly hostile
Die functionally
Die logically
Die automated
Die a landscape
Die an auxiliary
Die dispensable
I wish I could
Die lacking a tongue
Die at first sight unnerving
Die indexed
Die a surface
Die a curlicue
Die a syndrome
Die ascetic

A measure of merit
In every death I died
Die therefore my own
Die in seventeen minutes
Die cheaply and carelessly
Die gaudy and extreme
I wish I could die a mismatch of reason
Die empirical fact
Die naked and difficult
Die in Salzburg
Die in Warsaw
Die in Oslo
I wish I could die running
Die static
Die a hermit
Die a lover
Die a mirror
Die a futurist
Die like a large glass,
A glimpse into hell —
But no.

The Consecration of Spring;
A failure. Has to turn up lights.
Manager of theatre takes means
To stop hostile demonstrations
As dance goes on.

It took all the space I could turn on.
All the protein of a violently subdued thought.
What exactly *is* contingent, what is one half
Of what? Too late.
I've seen you now.

Howling by numbers, urgent staccato
Yelping, restrained; yanked by the coattails
On your wooden plinth,
A picture of pagan boyhood;
The divine masculine
From two feet above. Tears in your eyes
As she dances herself to death.
A single chord kills her.

The unparalleled tension
Of musical language,
We have all danced things
We have wanted to kill.

I was unprepared for the explosion.
I left the hall in a rage.
Life is communal
And depersonalised.

IV.

THE REALITY

Empty Signifier

A glass of water is what you need,
If only to hide that coffee ring

On a newspaper you'd never read
But someone at a party
Recommended the editorial
And now you live in fear that they,
Amongst a mob of nihilists,
Are just over your shoulder.

The only words you can make out are:
"Lifted", "special", "pilot" and "axiomatic";
See my horoscope on the back page:
"You didn't get what you asked for, Aries.
Does that make you ashamed?"
An excess of artefacts, perfectly silent.
Does that answer your question?

A cup of raisins is what you need;
A Mother Raw Earth figurine,
An embroidered apron, a reliable mirror,
Sometimes you act and speak
As if you've never actually seen one.
Don't: commerce,
Rail-road, banish.
Do: white flags, book-ends,
Balance beams –

The mind is a muscle and the dancer
Is a neutral, non-expressive doer;
When I think of you I'm only practicing

Form over a barre, tell me that a tutu
And a leotard is what I need, one click away
From perfect elegance; performance,
Roses at my feet, and adulation.
That's what I need.

I'm a talker, not a doer.
Not a dancer, barely a thinker.
Cynical narrators are what I need
When expression meets procrastination.
He is silent, a mosaic, intimidated and bloody.
You are cloudy, drowsy, opaque, pervious,
And somehow still dehydrated.

Frescoes, daisies, sinking ships,
Rites and prayers and cataclysms,
What if legs were pistons?
And we're powered by oil, and
Each of our limbs are just, just, just...
Utensils, or... *units*, or...

Mechanical processes aren't all bad
Just look at how they make diamonds.
But I will burn very much to death,
A volcanic death, the world's *worst* death
In hyperbole, when really, all I'd like to say is:

A glass of water is what you need.
If you see an overcast underpass,
Tell *nobody*, and wait, whilst I have you —

Please, just throw that newspaper away.
For everybody's sake.

Artefacts 1-13

The words "Christian Dior" on a glass bauble.
I put it on my wrists and started to worry: "And if the acoustic feedback eats into the dance? And if the fun can't rescue my nerve? And if the tension of the admiration meets... an enchanting function, or reality?"
Painting myself with lipstick. Folds of skin, moles and freckles. Sometimes I intellectualise what I should feel instead of feeling it.

A bus window through the city.
Video clips as Scythian vision. Remember, this journey is about massed energy. I feel, in this rehearsal mode, more human than ever before. I nearly can't handle the phase. No motor, no impulse for dance movement.

Your name on the wall.
Possible interpretations of the press release. The distance between the artist and his work.

A focus on the body.
Strangely nuanced, even undermined, in these idiosyncratic circumstances. The tie of sex with G-d is far stronger than the tie of wit, though everyone in the audience, except me, may try to have you believe otherwise. Convulsions of a will more vast. Accomplishing a rite — sitting for the whole of the thing. Completely caught and overwhelmed as the spectator.

Folk material as a speaker.
And I sat there and just looked at you and thought about how I was honoured to be near you and how I may always feel honoured to be near you. I hoped so.

The red of a Hockney.
An ancient other nestling in the heart of my divided soul today. As ancient as my own reality. Like a flock of birds on the wing, deviations in speech give texture, but do not disrupt the general pattern of what you're saying.

A crime against grace.
Do I seem to be breathing a bit too mysteriously before your very eyes? You do, probably. I'll be impersonal, evolutionist, whatever it is I said I would be. You can evoke blindness and think of animals circling in a cage, the mind/body split. You have no organ other than your entire organism, and it is with this that you search. Probably.

A terrifying range.
The question of whether your invocation of primitivism today was deliberate, and if so, has it brought about any kind of premature specimen of people like you in the future? Things like this call for the colourful and picturesque, but this is prehistoric romantic immediacy, and ultimately, fascism.

The nobility of a pint glass.
Fights and flirtations. Laughing and lamenting circles. Spirals. Simultaneous solos. First night patrons. Possessed woman. Young man. Young people. Tall woman in mauve. Vertical false relations. I don't know what else to say, I'm bad at this with you. I'm laughing though, it's your round. Panic terror which accompanies the rising of the sap.

A favourite nerve.
A conclusion unimaginable a decade earlier, a spring renewal as a metaphor for revolution. The intelligentsia await *approaching events*, and my thoughts turn to *unofficial venues*. Becoming affiliated with the local soundscape far more deeply than the part of me who breathlessly greeted these high elations could have imagined.

A struggle.
An attention in my middle that can't suit the struggle. This is the natural festival of the soul, the joy of self-sacrifice, not under the knife, nor exuberant in spirit. An array of pitches, the beautiful agitations of the psyche. As I said, a struggle.

An unlawful consideration.
Immense code. Some of these dances are like the frescoes of the Sistine Chapel's Last Judgement, "they dance the Earth out" to the genius of what love is. This is the kind of associative thinking that I can appreciate in the comparative mythological and romantic works such as the one that you, the subject, are reading and that I, the author, am writing.

An admittance of honey.
Ageing bodies articulating different experiences in the accumulated history of their movements. A plea in unbroken melodic flow of quarters and quick 5/4 meter, and again, largely in rapid, even quarter notes. Is it normal to think like this?

The more constraints we impose, the more we free ourselves of the chains that shackle the spirit. The arbitrariness of the constraint only serves to obtain precision of our execution, just like a letter I can never send, because this is not a fantasia, this is not a fantasia *yet* —

This is Normal

After Soundcarriers

Elevation and auditions,
Do not look the boy in the eye.
You are now ready to speak,
Relax; this is normal.

Hire an army
For a five-second gun siege
To split the silence;
This is normal.
The apology you almost made
Is now defeated.

Ellipses. Laughter. Aggrandisement.
It's painless. When you are in a fit state,
Add a loophole. You are now ready
To become obscene once more;
Send it as a telegram.
Add up your losses.
Specify what you aspire to,
But only if the goal is indecent.

Reform your aspirations
To include flimsy justifications.
Just try it out.
You are capable of being
A very beautiful brat.
It's now time to accept emergency.
Receive yourself, breathe in
And read the letter I wrote.
This is normal.

From Scenes of Pagan Russia (With Love)

Dear Vaslav,

I return and this time I bring glory. I lie with chaos and breathe. Extending yourself into space again, I see? It's like you're pushing me to show me you're not afraid of me, but from the inside of a switch cupboard. 59 times over I have felt this chord with the motor pulse, the motor pulse so emphatically: my head flung back and dropped forward, my eye-line off-balance and my sense of direction blurred. Russia was pregnant with revolution and you are still a miracle, Nijinsky. Personally I believe this liberating magic should be no different for men.

There's a place where harmony changes, and where you triumph over the art. I conceive of us in parallel. If you walk slowly, I'll walk slowly. Desire washes my conscience, so Vaslav — escape now from the chord and begin to move. It should be easy for you to break up the movement, and bring it back to a simple gesture. Keep in mind that to me, you feel partly rhapsodic.

The melody takes over, and accents disappear. When reading the score, you can see everything that's coming, but when we happen in time, you will only be able to guess the movement on the basis of what you have heard, or how familiar you are with the composer. You will read these great architectural shapes, but only now I ask you feel the dance as it rises in you. Dance with me the war. The war which we eventually conceded we could not prevent.

The renewal after us, is that a romance? The absurdity of such a renewal, is that a comedy? Or dancing to death because we lack the inner will to escape the sacrifice, is that a tragedy? Or, to put it differently, does the cycle of loss and renewal built into our repertoire inspire continuous reinvention? You are smiling, wound with pearls, with all the stuff of perversity the dawning century's imagination could provide, although there is a shapely dance without me, toward the end the chord generates a melody, your expressive sophistication — we are pure patterning. The aesthetic of the ballet body, my Vaslav. The direct attention before me. The ecstatic reconciling of the artist and the animal. Have you ever even been there? Would you like to go there now?

We perform a long arabesque. I follow your progress with my eyes. We move in and out, kneeling and rising, our hands at our waists, or our hands at the the sky, flayed fingers and two-footed jumps. A controversial masterpiece, that's what I instantly saw you as — if you were the Afternoon of a Faun, I would be jealous of the scarf.

We can be canonical. We can be distorted, enriched, revised and heavily romanticised, an unadulterated masterwork, an impure hybrid, a bastardised form. I am taking your pure music, I am making it riotous, broken, and purer still. Let me project my complex onto you, be your disruptive glory. Our landscape of regions as of yet untouched by civilisation. Spring rounds. Augurs. Rituals and glorification. Ancient Russian poetry. The ambiguity of it all.

I have to leave it here, it should be obvious as to why. I will appear to you as a gold watch, emblazoned with the eagle. Your name three times, and now say mine; Vaslav, Vaslav, Vaslav.

From scenes of pagan Russia (with love), Gospozha. x

Yarila

after Sergey Gorodetsky

The alleged habit sparks the war
Disgusting sugar gathered; three then four
Showers undertaken on the shore.
There where striking worry briefs the poems,
Whitening strips so I can say them wide
And then dental repair from eating pride;
The war of words.
Sweet and naked.

An impeccable shape on the beach,
Standard as an adamant arrest;
Said over two-thousand moons, addressed
Just like a pigeon breast
Tastes something like a heart,
The beach of your dark something
Trains apart.

At the shingle, there we sit sketching
And draft The Rite of Spring,
I fantasise,
I eulogise,
Consequences start to unionise
Quite far and wide
Like the water, our stomachs bright.

One I took, one I led,
Adamant and softly said: "Eat the sand".
And profuse, like a kiss,
A condition arose

And then died.
The meal that made me quite hysterical.

I could healthily withdraw my tooth.
I could be the sun,
You could sweep the sun,
Or split it once,
Or join it twice;
Fiercely cleaving.

The likeness is too close
To be coincidental.
Animals pass by.
I could eat the sun,
Or split it once,
Or join it twice,
If my decisions try
To hold me heavenly
And tightly flawed,

In the red sand will lie
Two new gods.

Glorification

I never thought that I would see
A poltergeist as lovable as you.

In the bluebell flare of friendship,
Lampshades fall to mute the limits;
Blacklight strips in cottages
To stop us shooting up.

Flashbacks patterned with landmarks:
A landfill of bombs, skysails housing
Lovers, eggshells, lambskins, egos
In every lozenge orange window –
I can only guess.

A wrong turn, a ruled pavement
Portioned up to limbo towpaths;
A hologram of you stood
Half an inch over the line.

I never thought that I would meet
A spectacle as still as you.

Like a clairvoyant eyewitness
Holding his breath
For the robbery.

Ostinato

I care if you listen. The classics are ours. The basic line of music. Dialogues. Developments. Astonish me. Only art promises mortality. I'll wait for you to astound me. Madness is true of the normal heart. I'm severely afraid of dying in water. So many moments of happiness and anguish. I became nervous. I will eat everyone. I am man's firstborn. The murmurs endowed. Sit before the Alps, then picture the Himalayas. Do one thing. A common and sincere language: the Rite of Spring.

I'm there if you listen. The classical hours. The baseline of music. A dial-up envelopment. Astonish me. Only art promises morality. I'd hate for you to astound me. Madness is true of the formal heart. I'm severely ashamed of dyeing the water. So many moments of happiness in language. You'll become serviced. I will cheat everyone. I am man reborn in the fervour of crowds. I sit before the Alps, scripture the Himalayas. Do nothing. A common and austere language: the height of things.

Beware if you listen, the farcical hours. The hate crime of music, in spite of the strings. I care if you leaf through a catalogue. I'm there if you grieve a development. Admonish me. Lonely starts premise insanity. I'll wait for you to confound me. Gladness is true of a subnormal heart. I'm clearly ashamed of trying the water; so many moments of kidnapping language. Before our civil service I will cheat, hit and run. I am a dialogue, an excessive experiment. I am man stillborn. The brochure for shrouds. Sit before the Alps, write scripts for your players. Dialogues do nothing. Developments examine an unclear language: it's the hindsight that stings.

In prayer if you listen, the traffic is ours, it's the hate crime of losing to dialogues/developments in the light of all things, in prayer if you listen, I care if you listen with honesty in lonely hours; I'd miss the you of me. I'd hate for you to surround me. Sadness is you with a powder-horn heart. I'm nearly untamed when I'm close to the water, so many warnings from unwrapping language, before I do it disservice I tweet, hit and run. Fever is now. Be gripped unawares. Do something the night that we premier the playwright's new fling, a socialite sings a new prayer if you listen to dialogues. Beware if you hasten developments. Don't swear off a vision as dialogue. I care if you listen, repetitive stamping, no pattern of accent; the woodwind, percussion, the brass and the strings, just *sit down now*.

I care if you listen. Do one thing. A common and sincere language: The Rite of Spring.

Artefacts 100-113

The words: "leave in for 20-40 minutes to achieve the desired result" written on the side of a box of blue-black hair dye.
It was then the reflection found variety in every hair strand. Something sordid about how my hair drinks it. Ease doesn't cheat the pattern. You can't expect sharpness to be met with patience.

A birds-eye view of empathy.
If you can hear the bell but not identify it, that's your problem. A wistful negotiation can't also be an electric stop sign; a marvellous rush is an elite emergency, only the very pretty get to feel it. You can't be a communist when it comes to desire. I really can't put it any clearer than that.

Your name on the screen.
Possible interpretations of the fact that the closer your eye gets to a computer screen, the more any word can look like a game of Tetris. Love looks like Tetris. Hello looks like Tetris. Today's a fucking nightmare looks like Tetris. Imagine if you wrote the word Tetris and I wrote the word Tetris and by the end of it we're just playing Tetris; where would that leave us? And I guess I mean "us" on a global scale, but I also mean "us" as in, y'know. Us.

A focus on the temporal.
An untrue week. Strangely distinct, even in these unchanging windows. The tie of sex breaks across the heresies needed in order to prevent innovations from becoming fixed as orthodoxies. It feels like a regression into blindness, completely caught and overwhelmed by a primitive dissociation. I just keep saying, "The Rite of Spring, The Rite of Spring". I can just say it. I can just say, "The Rite of Spring".

Folk material as a gambit.
Parisian modernity from changing vantage points, I dunno. Arresting and unfamiliar sounds and spectacles ranging from rapt attention, to laughter and catcalls. This was at the premiere, you weren't there but I can sum it up for you: "Authentic artist encounters a profound unhappiness and thus becomes inauthentic and ultimately, a fascist". That's the headline, take it or leave it.

The black of a typeface.
I will tell you I never saw it if it makes things easier for you. I'll even make you believe it. You'll forget it was a lie.

A crime against attachment theory.
It's time for honesty: I'm dismissive-avoidant. Oral-aggressive. A dark triad woman (or anything else) figuring into the asymmetry of my own destruction. I am in this position or that one, I claim a stereotypical account of what constitutes a narcissist from a deeply utopian position. Acts of horrible brutality, an insane perpetrator, see me: a terrifying range.

A terrifying range.
Whatever your aesthetic position, what matters is your engagement with the contemporary world, and your rejection of the conventions of the past, and how this implies some retroactive scandal. The Rite will be the thing that proves your centrality to one's memory. Resistance as a means of defying the ephemeral nature of dance through continual reinvention, and *furthermore* — fuck me, you're gorgeous. Did you know that? Sorry. Of course you did.

The concern of a long-stem wine glass.
Referring to my old notes, I now have to ask myself what I thought I meant when I implied a circle could be lamented. Horizontal false relations has a more salacious ring to it, though in context it still means nothing at all. Small blue sedatives like a fizz-bomb sublingually. A goldfinch is a person who loves to dress up smartly and carefully.

A favourite nerve.
A conclusion unimaginable. By which I mean, I can't imagine anything I've ever been, am now, or ever will be. That's not your responsibility though. Only you are your own responsibility, and I think even then that's a whole... *thing*. You should try becoming affiliated with your local soundscape, go to an anechoic chamber and listen to the swooshing of your blood pressure, the buzzy screech of your nervous system. Because I'm not going to do it for you, I simply do not have the means.

A struggle.
Please don't die in the anechoic chamber, there are all sorts of precautions you can take. I once saw a documentary about the most humane way to execute a serial killer, and what they found was you should starve the brain of oxygen, which feels quite nice in the

beginning. Delirious, euphoric, even. The subject* they used for this theory found it hard to want to leave when the experiment reached a near fatal point. For what it's worth I've never actually been to an anechoic chamber but I feel like it's not a million miles away from what I just described. Just keep perspective in there. I know you will. (*Michael Portillo. Eager to die. Who knew?)

An inductive consideration.
It's me, I'm goldfinch.

A cryptogram.
I'd like to thank Igor Stravinsky; Sergei Diaghilev; Nicolas Roerich; and you, Vaslav; Greta who sold me the beautiful fake mink coat; Freda who reupholstered said coat with pink silk lining; pink silk lining as a metaphor for the inside of an ear; a diamond stud; the Royal Northern College of Music for their performance of Different Trains by Steve Reich in 2011; the uniquely Russian voice; the uniquely Jewish voice; twelve professors; conflicting Hebrew transliterations of The Sh'ma; the original composers of the songs I almost played on the janky old guitar in the corner right there; my first marriage; the French titles of different sections; the book you wrote indirectly about schizophrenia; the diagnosis you incorrectly made of sociopathy; the following two symposia: *"Drinking in the Afternoon: an Inaugural Conference"* held in the smallest version of Minsk I've ever lived in; and *"How Did I Get Here? And Who With?"*, held in some place I really can't go back to any more which is a shame because it wasn't such a bad place and holds a lot of sentimental value but then again so do you, so, you see my problem.

You'll notice that the inclination for automated procedures is not so much mercifully rigid as it is a lot like falling face down onto a bed and breathing into the pillow, the things only things to be said can easily be reduced to nostalgic gutturals and safe words. Creative manipulations can be dismantled but, from experience, they will keep dismantling and, however neatly, it will still look as if a landmine was here. To be candid for a second (and I think I've earned the right), it literally feels like a landmine was here. Dinosaurs hulking over the mountain now and I'm one of them. But this is not a fantasia. This is not a fantasia *yet* —

Tulpa

A tulpa is an embodiment of such wish, desire, longing and/or love that it has become a sentient being in its own right — willed into existence by deep emotion, and no longer controllable by its creator(s).

And his name is Vaslav Nijinsky.
This genius would follow each person
From the hour of their birth
Until the moment of their death;
Smoky at the bedside like toothache,
Euphonic as laughter, but silent.

I know what you're thinking but a glow *can* be sharp,
And If you'd ever held an ammonite the sea hadn't got to,
You'd know that.
So I can say that the tulpa we made
Is radiance with teeth and a coke-nail.

Magnetars have unmannerly viciousness.
Breathing in is ridiculous and out is flamboyant.
My Vaslav is your Vaslav, what's mine is yours
So you are now the proud owner of a bouquet of clovers,
A flower but unsound, a mammal but fascinated
Because we fascinated him —
But let's give thanks to G-d that he's beautiful.

The rose-coloured gurgling can be heard in the valley,
Don't listen to who tells you it's a death-rattle, or grey,
And the pirouetting intellect inside that uproar
Will go mad. He'll go frighteningly mad.
And we'll have to watch him,
My hand in your hand.

This tulpa has become an infamy to me.
I have nestled in Vaslav's pockets,
Waited in Vaslav's wings and lived
In Vaslav's splintered landscapes, hipped
My shins to Vaslav's calves and put my
Hand over his mouth; we have loved his
Body between us, safer that way —
You don't know it, but you have a stake
In his grace.

I have read his diaries and held a pillow,
Vaslav's pillow, the Nijinsky grip,
"I am not crying but I have tears in my heart";
I think we are those tears, I think we
Therefore should be left alone
To gamble on the Stock Exchange,
Grieve, and do everything love commands us to.
Nijinsky hadn't the words to make the laws
For learning to wait in the air, he said:
"I merely leap and pause".
Healthy men rebuking their sick neighbours,
Vaslav moved into what we think
Might be our neighbourhood

And in our circling antiheroic undoings
Because sometimes that's what love is;
Fresh developments and influences from Moscow —
The Russian revolution: Limerence.
The eve of war: First night nerves.
The White Star Line: Go to the pharmacy?
The Rite of Spring: I love you.

It's often just enough to be with someone,
You don't need even need to touch them, or talk.
A feeling passes between you both —
You are not alone.

His name is Vaslav Nijinsky
And we let him come to the conclusion
That it's better to be silent than speak,
But then he danced appalling things
Far beyond our control.

And he thinks the earth will be like Mars
But in a few hundred years hence;
He has us looking for just one small universe
In which only secrets can survive.

Vaslav Nijinsky, my one big truth —
You are a work of art.
I'm sorry I got it as wrong as I did;

This *is* a fantasia.

Note on the Text

Vaslav Nijinksy (12th March 1889 - 8th April 1950) was a Polish born ballerino and choreographer, widely regarded to be the greatest dancer of his generation, perhaps even of all time. His ability to embody any role given to him and to choreograph works in completely new and sometimes controversial ways earned him the title of genius, and he is still held in such high esteem today. He is most noted for his innovative and arguably modernist choreographies for *L'Après-midi d'un faune, Jeux*, and of course, *The Rite of Spring*, a work he fully choreographed, but in which he did not dance.

He was shrouded in mystery and adored by many, rumours about him were wild and elaborate. One such rumour was that Nijinsky had been having an affair with an Indian prince, who gifted to him girdles wrought with pearls and emeralds. Women, who had previously had no collective outlet for their sexual desire, would sneak backstage and steal his underwear. His masseuse would give people a rundown of his physique for a small fee, and when he danced *La Spectre de la rose* in 1911, the silk petals that fell off his costumes were sold as souvenirs. Artists, poets and composers alike often positioned him as a muse, and still do. Amongst them include Tennessee Williams, WH Auden, Edward Albee, Frank Stanford, Giorgos Seferis, and Auguste Rodin, who sculpted him in 1912 after becoming fascinated by his performance in Debussy's *L'Après-midi d'un faune.*

For *The Rite*, Nijinsky worked with Igor Stravinsky (the composer), Sergei Diaghilev (the impresario of The Ballet Russes), and Nicolas Roerich (the artist and set designer), referred to cynically by critics as The Four Idiots. His choreography itself was a destruction; undoing everything the dancers knew about ballet and starting again with previously unheard of and brutal, techniques, with dancers having complained of sprained ankles and snapped tendons. One critic said, with disdain, that his choreography was nothing but, "Knock-kneed Lolitas jumping up and down". Nijinsky's sister was replaced by another dancer when she fell pregnant during rehearsals as he did not want to cause a miscarriage.

At the premier of *The Rite of Spring*, a riot began within moments of the music beginning. The commotion was so loud that Nijinsky had to stand on a chair in the wings, shouting out numbers to the dancers on stage so they could keep time as they could no longer hear the orchestra. Stravinsky was holding him by the coat-tails to stop him from falling. Nijinsky had dressed in white-tie formal, believing he would be invited onto the stage to take a bow.

Unfortunately, Nijinsky was already showing warning signs of the psychosis. Having always been troubled, his mental health began to deteriorate; he would stop performances half-way through and leave, and became increasingly paranoid and hyper-religious. The pianist who accompanied one of his last performances was reported to have wept throughout. It could be *The Rite of Spring* that sparked his breakdown, or the fact he had been groomed by his mother to enter into relationships with older men in order to advance his career, or that Sergei Diaghilev was known to have sexually assaulted and abused him throughout their relationship. Nijinsky ended up losing his lucidity for good, and was eventually diagnosed with chronic schizophrenia. He was taken to the Bellevue Sanatorium in Zurich in 1919 after the birth of his daughter Kyra, and spent the rest of his life in institutions.

He died on the 8th of April, 1950, at the age of 61, and was buried in London, though his body was moved in 1953 and reinterred in Montmartre Cemetery in Paris.

No film exists of Vaslav Nijinsky dancing.

Acknowledgements

I give thanks to all the friends who listened to my voice notes and read the screenshots of these poems in their various inceptions, at antisocial hours; their invaluable advice and encouragement.

I give thanks to Professor Thomas Forrest Kelly for his inspiring lectures on The Rite of Spring and therefore for introducing me to The Boy Himself, having had no idea of what he was starting in me.

I give thanks to Leanne Bridgewater, for the force and beauty of her talent, who wrote, "a cracked mirror in a glass vase" in one of her poems that I saw her perform nine years ago, the brevity and beauty of which stuck with me the whole time I was writing this book. In that respect, I give thanks that although she is technically no longer here, it doesn't mean she is no longer here. I give thanks that she lived here on earth with us, and that her poetry still does.

I give thanks to all of my mishpachah at Jacksons Row Synagogue, Manchester, to dear Rabbi Robyn, and dear Rav Reuven. I give thanks to Jack Adam Morris for helping me out with the Hebrew translation, and the warmth of his Jewish soul.

I give thanks to Kitty Seeney for her outpouring of support, love, advice and recognition — one who is so loving, she ought to be famous.

I give thanks to G-d and thanks to all Creation.

And I must give thanks to the strength of feeling which emerged when I wrote this manuscript, where it took me; through Vaslav I danced the horror and beauty of the things our hearts make us do, forever or never, leaping and pausing.

Baruch Attah Adonai Eloheinu melech ha'olam, meshaney habriyot.

This was real.

Ballet Out Your Unrest

www.ingramcontent.com/pod-product-compliance
Lightning Source LLC
Chambersburg PA
CBHW022122040426
42450CB00006B/812
* 9 7 8 1 9 1 5 0 7 9 2 9 9 *